LEARN TO READ

Sight Words STORYBOOK

25 Simple Stories & Activities for Beginner Readers

KIMBERLY ANN KIEDROWSKI

Illustrations by Claire Keay

ROCKRIDGE PRESS

For general information on our other products and services or to obtain technical support, please contact our Customer Care Department within the United States at (866) 744-2665, or outside the United States at (510) 253-0500.

Rockridge Press publishes its books in a variety of electronic and print formats. Some content that appears in print may not be available in electronic books, and vice versa.

Interior and Cover Designer: Francesca Pacchini
Art Producer: Samantha Ulban
Editor: Jeanine Le Ny
Production Editor: Andrew Yackira
Illustrations by © 2020 Claire Keay

ISBN: Print 978-1-64611-430-6 | eBook 978-1-64611-846-5

RO

Printed in Canada

Contents

Introduction

Learning sight words is one of the most important things to master as a new reader. Sight words are those that appear with great frequency in text. Many of these words do not follow phonetic rules. Therefore, children must automatically recognize them. In my 10 years of teaching kindergarten, I've seen how important it is for new readers to learn sight words and to have practice with them in print.

Children who learn sight words and apply them to their reading succeed in becoming strong and confident readers. With this in mind, it is important to practice using these sight words in different ways. One of the most effective ways is to use them while reading.

Your child must master sight words to become an independent, successful reader. Yet, learning to read sight words can be tricky. That's how this book can help. It has 25 cute stories and fun activities that feature 50 of the most common sight words. Each story focuses on two sight words. Two activities after each story will let your child practice these sight words. Working with sight words in these activities will help your child remember them.

Note to Parents

Use this book as a tool to help your child become a confident reader. With your guidance they will successfully learn 50 sight words. Sight words can be challenging to learn, but using this book weekly will give your child the knowledge necessary to become a strong reader.

Read the story aloud to your child and then find the sight words in the text together. On another day, have the child reread the story and trace the words. On a different day, have the child reread the story and complete the other activity. Finally, have your child read the story again. If your child can confidently read the words, continue on to the next story. As your child progresses through the book, each story will increase slightly in difficulty.

Remember that sight words often cannot be sounded out. If your child is trying to sound out one of these words, try going back and reviewing that word again. Point to it, say it, spell it, and then return to the story. If your child learns through movement, you may want to get rubber or magnetic letters and have them form the words. Allowing your child to finger write the words in shaving cream on a cookie sheet can be a fun reinforcement tool.

Here are a few more helpful tips to guide your child as they read through each story:

1. **Always review the featured sight words before reading.**
2. **Have your child search for the sight words before and after reading.**
3. **Have your child point to each word while reading.**
4. **Have your child use the pictures in the stories to help them figure out unknown words.**

These strategies, along with your support, will encourage your young reader to apply sight words in other forms of print throughout the day.

Finally, have fun! Learning sight words can be hard, but if you have fun with it, then your child will have fun with it, too!

I Like to Play

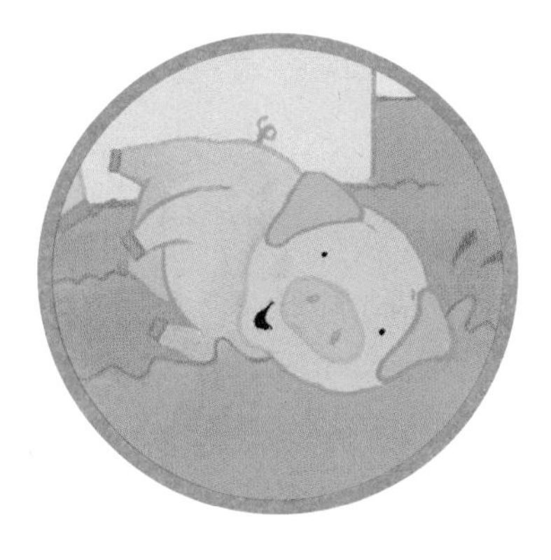

FOCUS SIGHT WORDS:

like, to

We like to play here.

We like to play here.

We like to play here.

We like to play here.

We like to play here.

We like to play here.

Activity Time

Say the word. Then, trace the word.

like like like like

like like like like

like like like like

Say the word. Then, trace the word.

to to to to to

to to to to to

to to to to to

Activity Time

Find and circle the word **like** three times.
Then, do the same for the word **to**.

a	b	a	g	l	a
t	o	t	r	i	o
e	p	o	y	k	f
t	l	i	k	e	m
u	h	b	s	z	a
l	i	k	e	t	o

A Day at the Park

FOCUS SIGHT WORDS:

up, down

We go up.

We go down.

We go up.

We go down.

We go up.

Oops! You go down.

Activity Time

Say the word. Then, trace the word.

up up up up up

up up up up up

up up up up up

Say the word. Then, trace the word.

down down down

down down down

down down down

Activity Time

Color each space that has the word **up** or **down**.

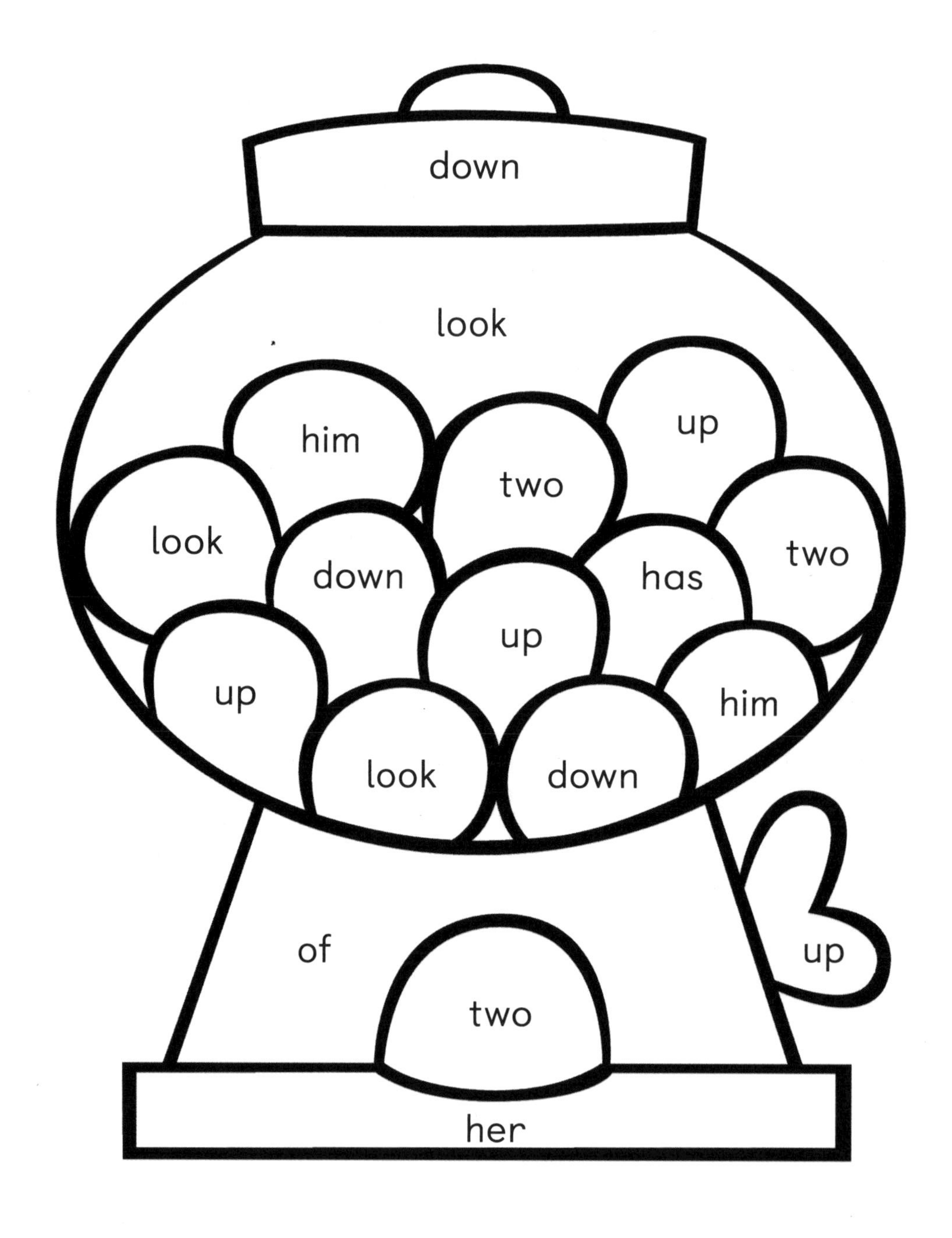

Let's Get Ready

FOCUS SIGHT WORDS:

a, little

A little **shirt.**

A little **sock.**

A *little* **shoe!**

A little **hat.**

A little **glove?**

A **big hug!**

Activity Time

Say the word. Then, trace the word.

a a a a a a

a a a a a a

a a a a a a

Say the word. Then, trace the word.

little little little

little little little

little little little

Activity Time

Color each circle that has the word **a** or **little**.
Then, follow the colored circles to complete the maze.

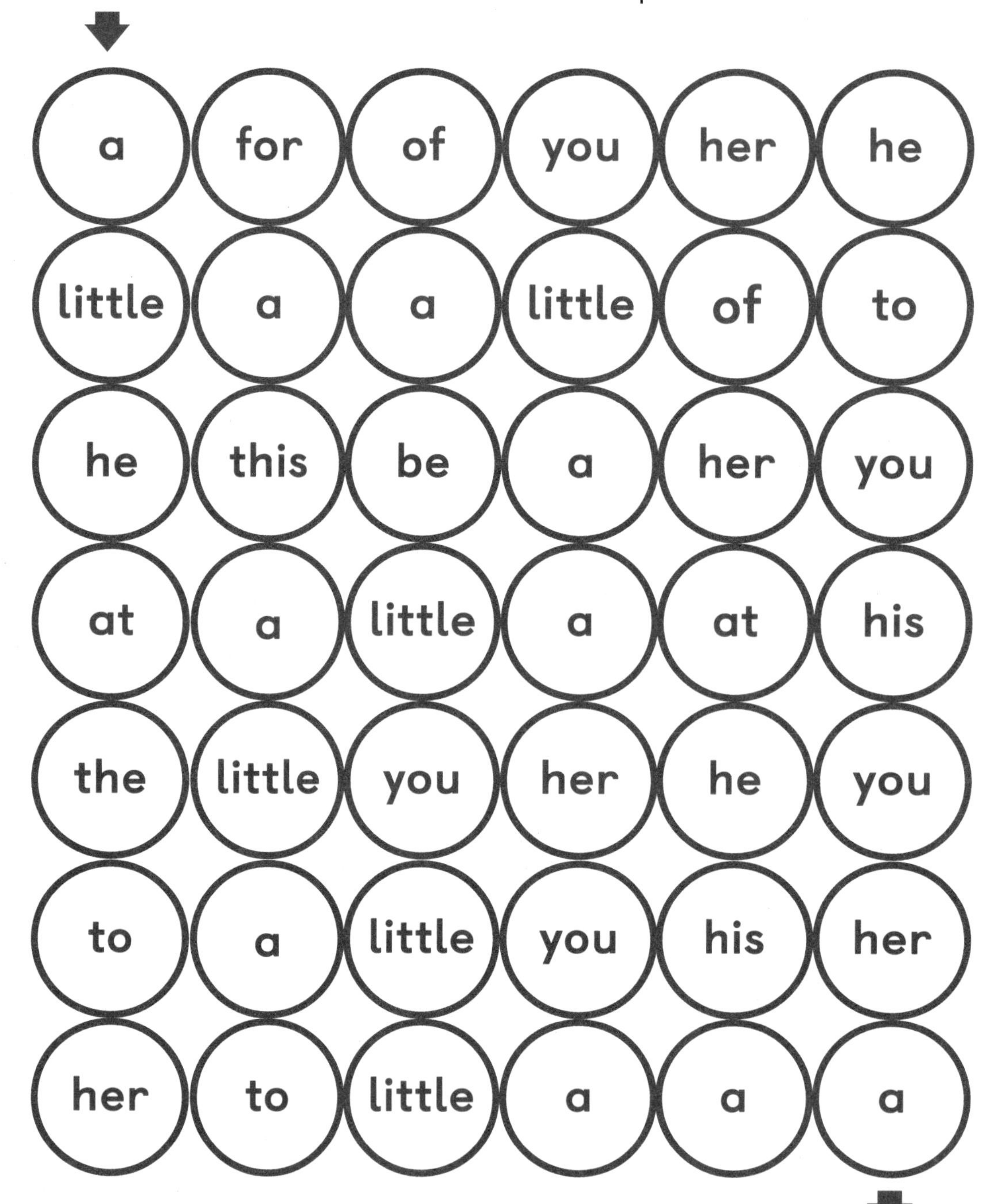

The Picnic

FOCUS SIGHT WORDS:

you, have

I have the plates.

You have the food.

I have the cups.

You have the juice.

I have the basket.

We have a picnic!

Activity Time

Say the word. Then, trace the word.

you you you you

you you you you

you you you you

Say the word. Then, trace the word.

have have have

have have have

have have have

Activity Time

Color each cherry that has the word **you** or **have**.

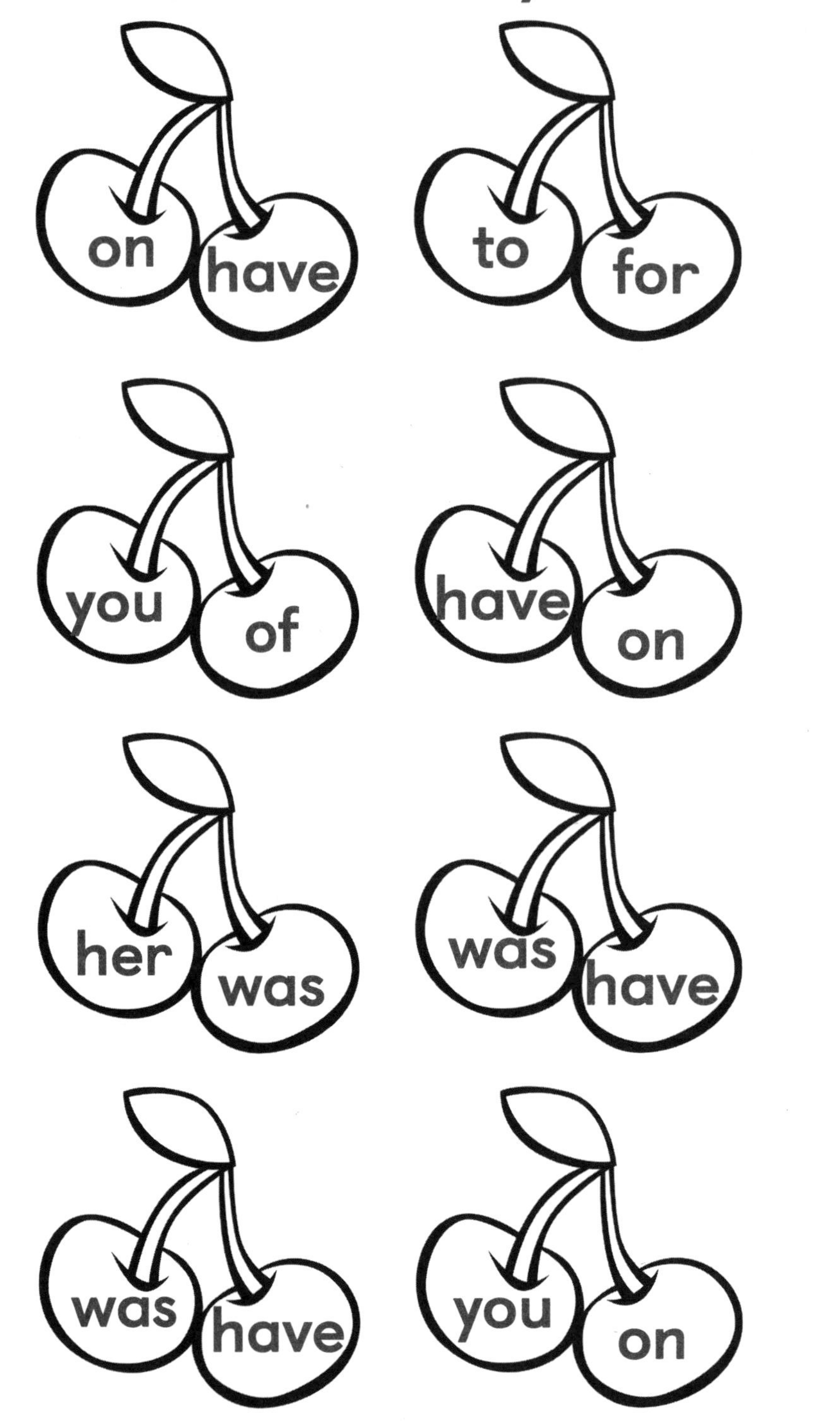

Helpful Me

FOCUS SIGHT WORDS:

help, my

I help my mom.

I help my dad.

I help my sister.

I help my grandma.

I help my grandpa.

They help me!

Activity Time

Say the word. Then, trace the word.

help help help

help help help

help help help

Say the word. Then, trace the word.

my my my my

my my my my

my my my my

Activity Time

Draw lines to connect the letters to form the word **help**.

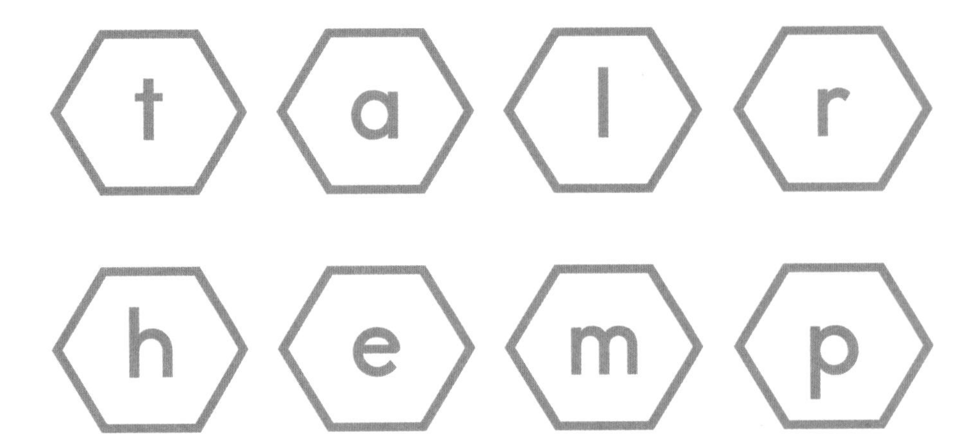

Draw lines to connect the letters to form the word **my**.

On the Farm

FOCUS SIGHT WORDS:

goes, the

The cow goes, "Moo."

The horse goes, "Neigh."

The **pig** goes, "**Oink.**"

The **hen** goes, "**Cluck.**"

The sheep goes, "Baa."

The farmer goes, "Shh!"

Activity Time

Say the word. Then, trace the word.

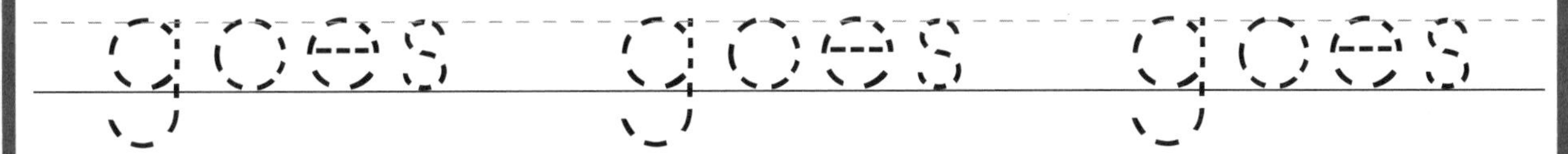

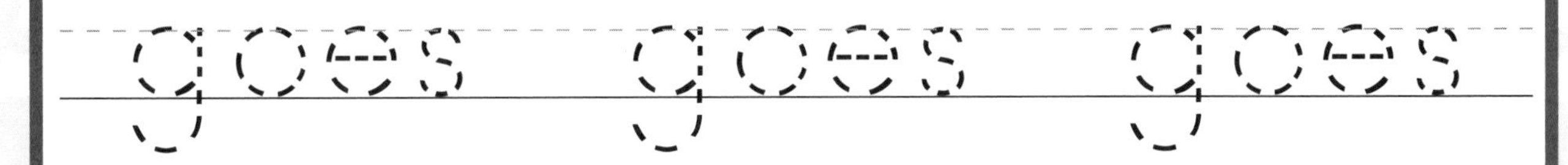

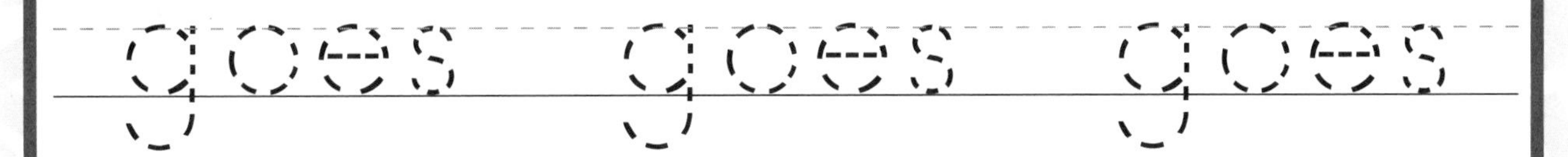

Say the word. Then, trace the word.

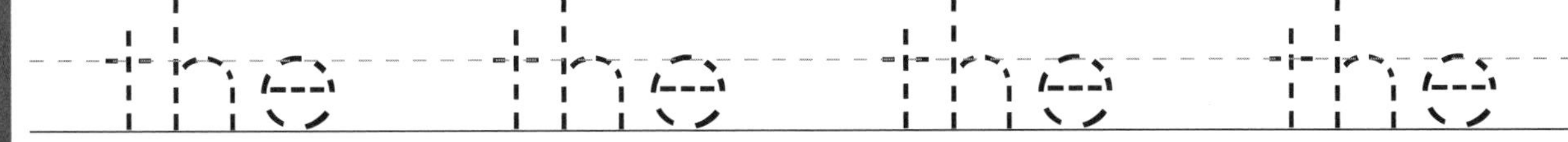

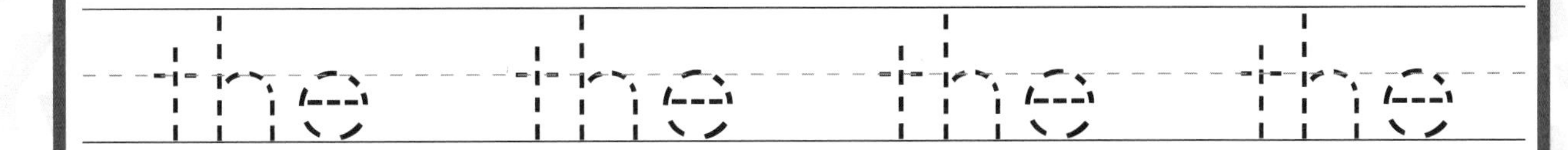

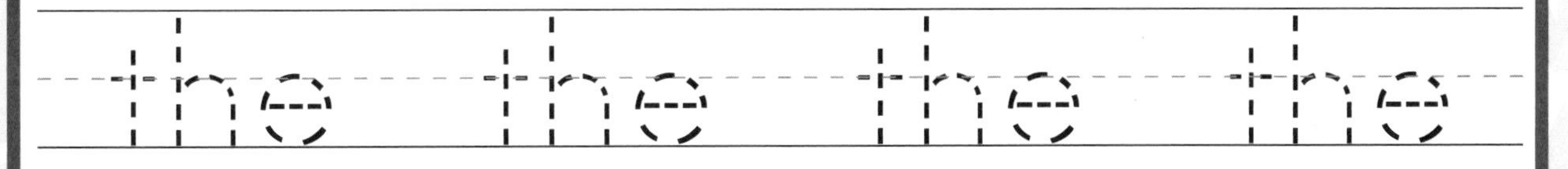

Activity Time

Find the word **goes**. Draw a line under each one.

Find the word **the**. Circle each one.

goes that of

the was

the it

on to on

for

at it on

goes was

at

on goes

her the

on

the of on

Jump In

FOCUS SIGHT WORDS:
jump, in

We jump in.

We jump out.

We jump in.

We jump out.

We jump in.

We do not jump out.

Activity Time

Say the word. Then, trace the word.

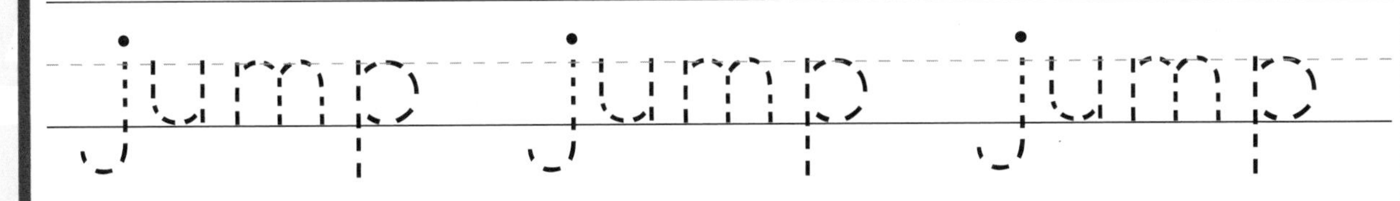

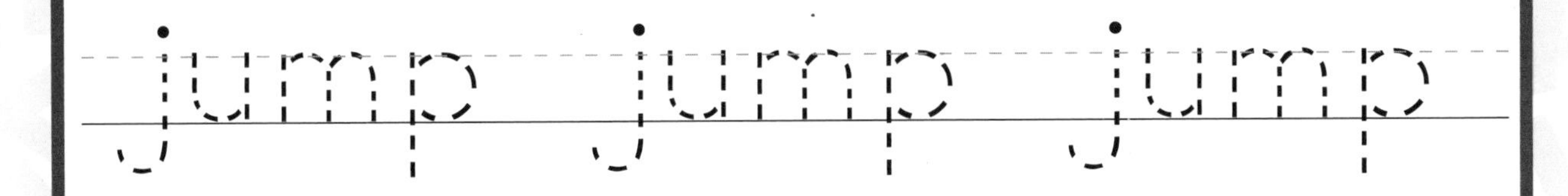

Say the word. Then, trace the word.

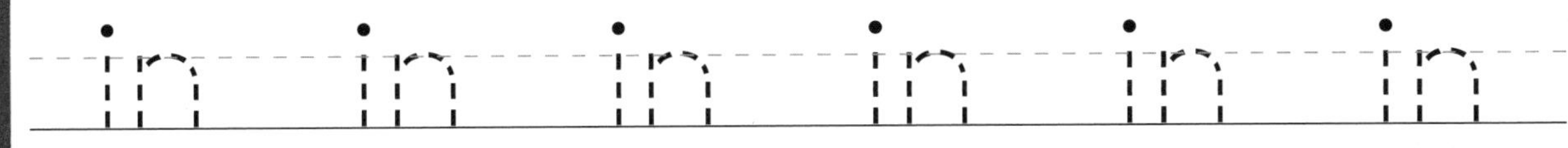

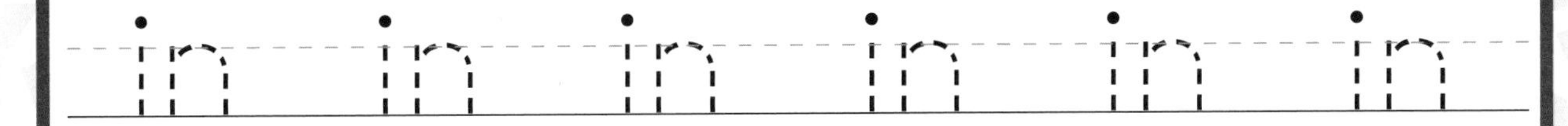

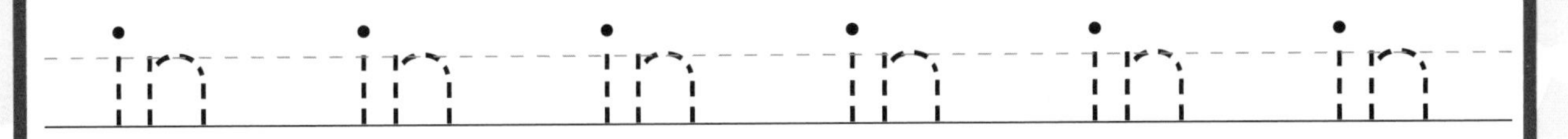

Activity Time

Color each space that has the word **jump** or **in**.

My Town

FOCUS SIGHT WORDS:

here, look

Look! The fire truck is here.

Look! The police car is here.

Look! The ambulance is here.

Look! The mail truck is here.

Look! The school bus is here.

Look at my town!

Activity Time

Say the word. Then, trace the word.

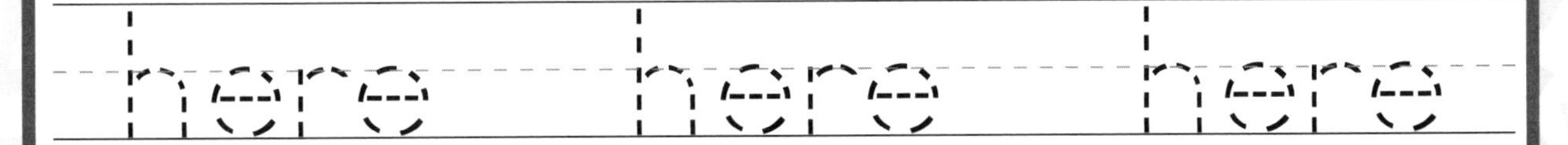

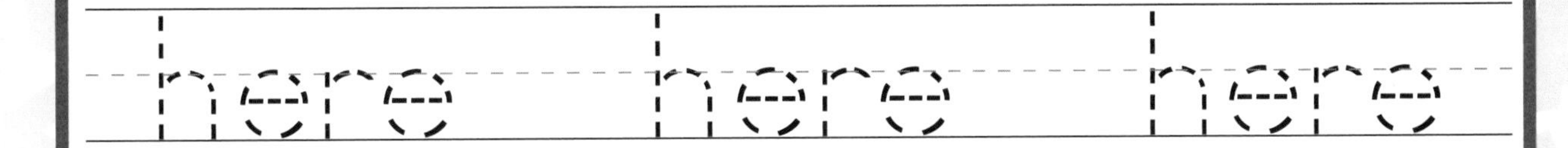

Say the word. Then, trace the word.

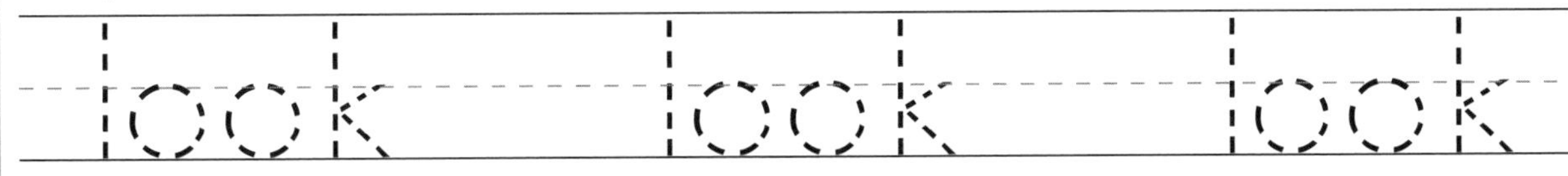

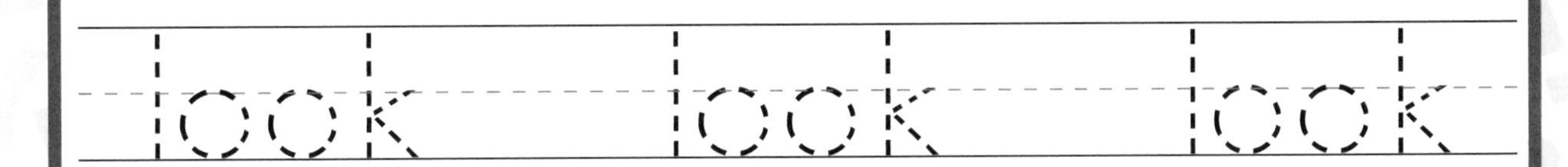

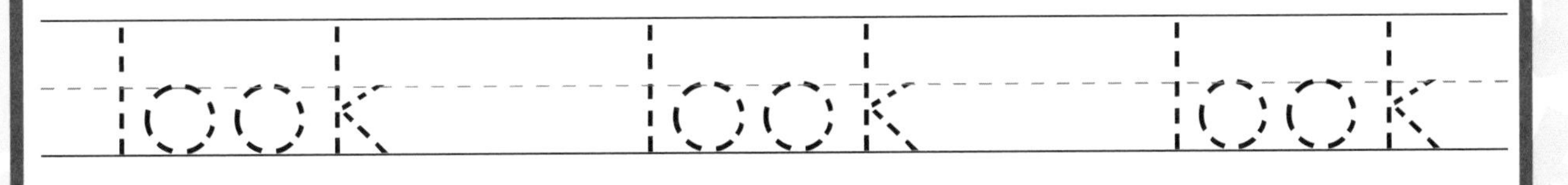

Activity Time

Color each circle that has the word **here** or **look**.
Then, follow the colored circles to complete the maze.

I Like Lots of Things

FOCUS SIGHT WORDS:

is, when

I like when it is sunny.

I like when it is windy.

I like when it is snowy.

I like when it is rainy.

I like when the sky is blue.

I like when I am with you.

Activity Time

Say the word. Then, trace the word.

is is is is is is

is is is is is is

is is is is is is

Say the word. Then, trace the word.

when when when

when when when

when when when

Activity Time

Color each plum that has the word **is** or **when**.

Hide and Seek

FOCUS SIGHT WORDS:

are, by

Where are you?

I am by the swings.

Where are you?

I am by the tree.

Where are they?

Here we are!

Activity Time

Say the word. Then, trace the word.

are are are are

are are are are

are are are are

Say the word. Then, trace the word.

by by by by by

by by by by by

by by by by by

Activity Time

Draw lines to connect the letters to form the word **are**.

Draw lines to connect the letters to form the word **by**.

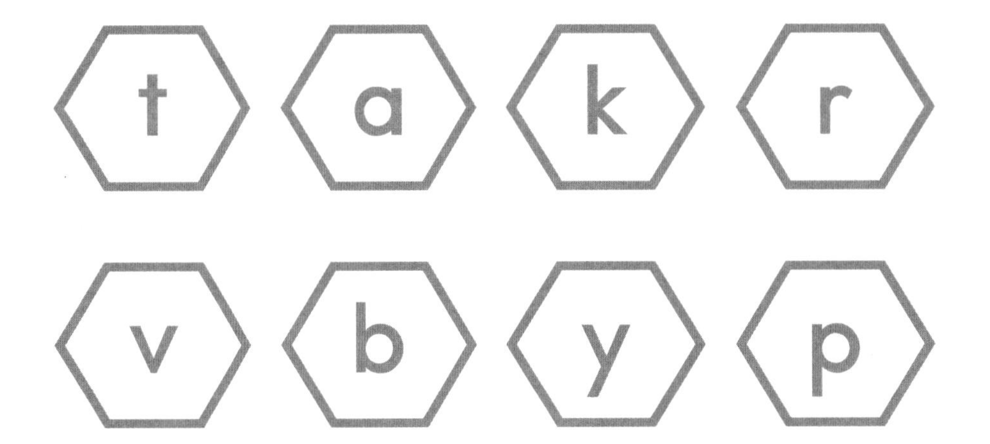

Let's Eat

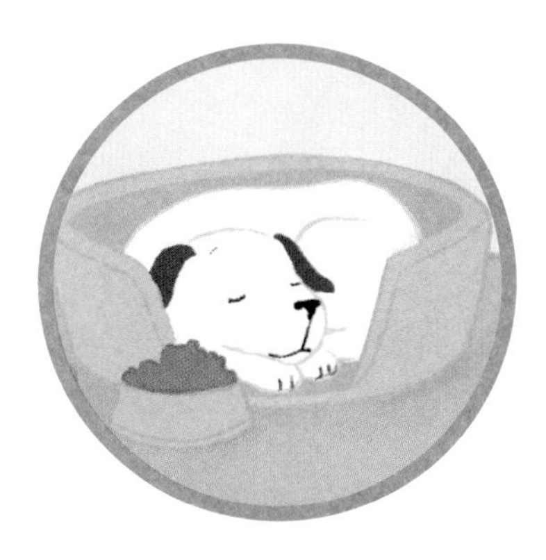

FOCUS SIGHT WORDS:

very, was

Dad was very **hungry.**

Mom was very **hungry.**

Sam was very hungry.

Pam was very hungry, too.

Time to eat.

Now, they are not very hungry.

Activity Time

Say the word. Then, trace the word.

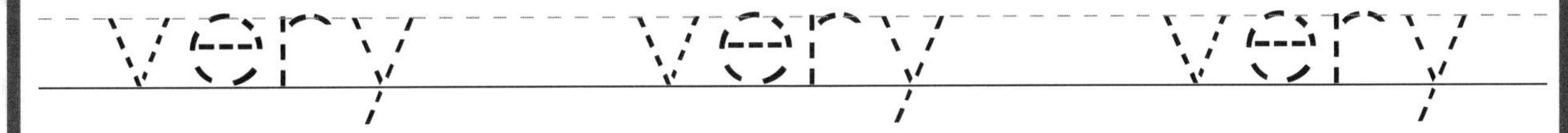

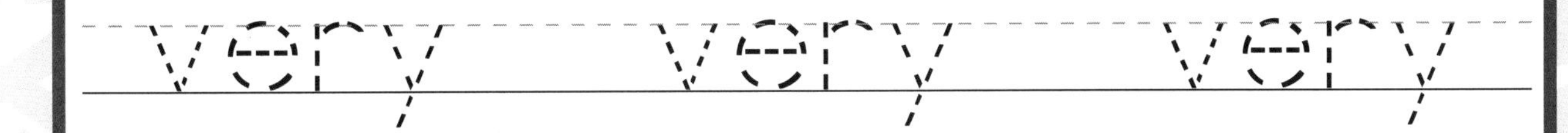

Say the word. Then, trace the word.

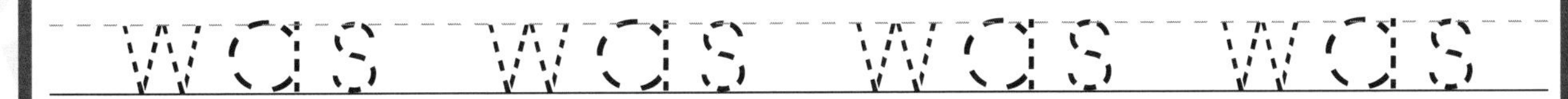

was was was was

Activity Time

Color each space that has the word **very** or **was**.

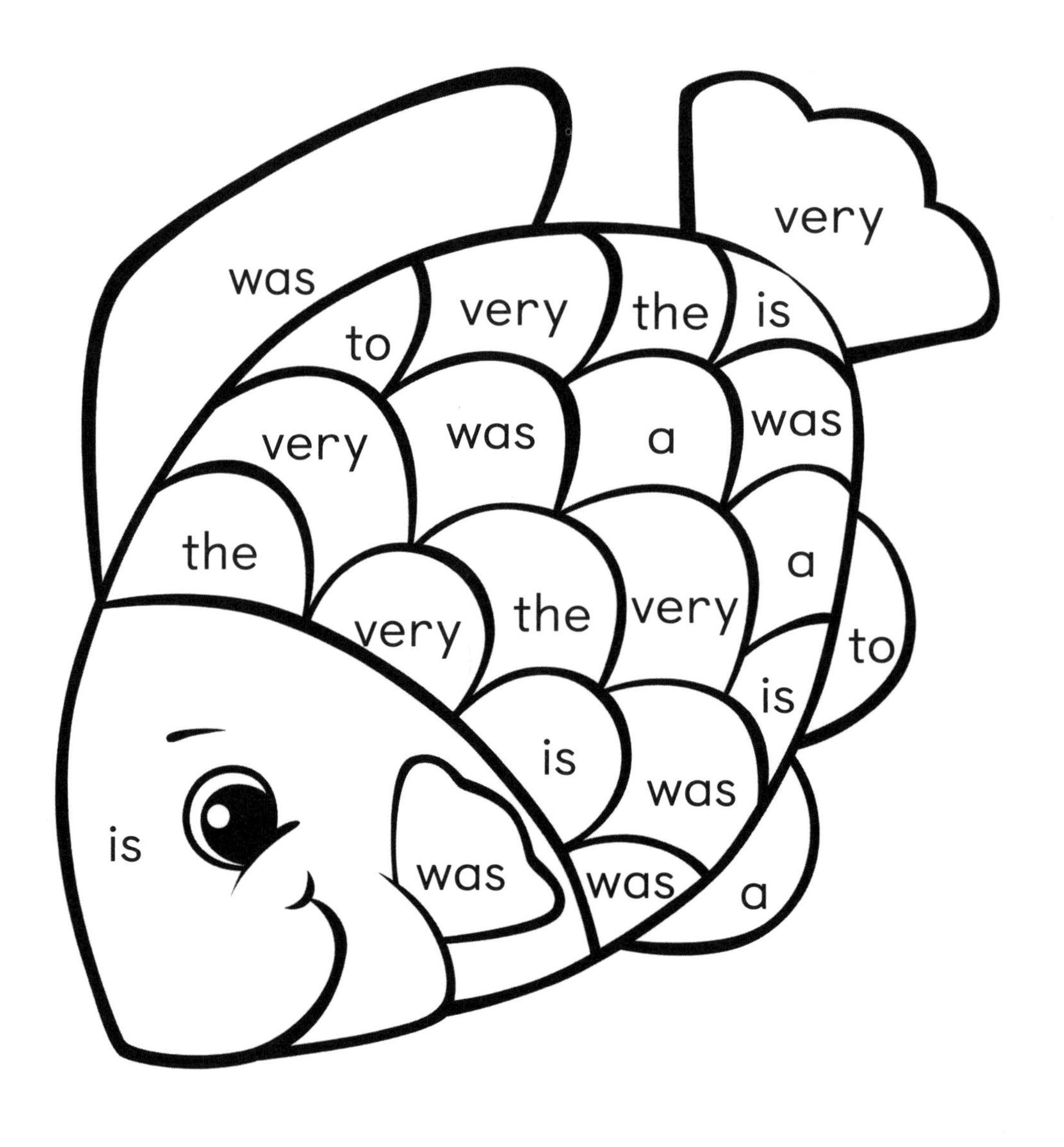

Pancakes

FOCUS SIGHT WORDS:

can, I

I can **scoop.**

I can **mix.**

I can **pour.**

I can **watch.**

I can **carry.**

I can **say, "Surprise!"**

Activity Time

Say the word. Then, trace the word.

can can can can

can can can can

Say the word. Then, trace the word.

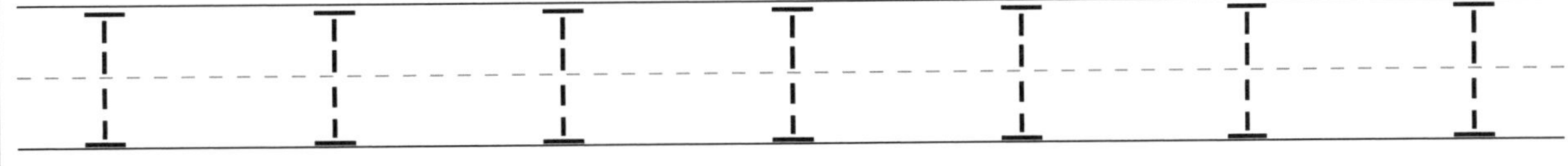

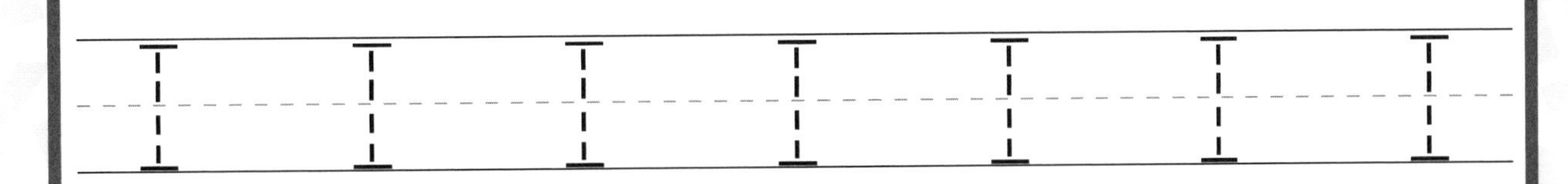

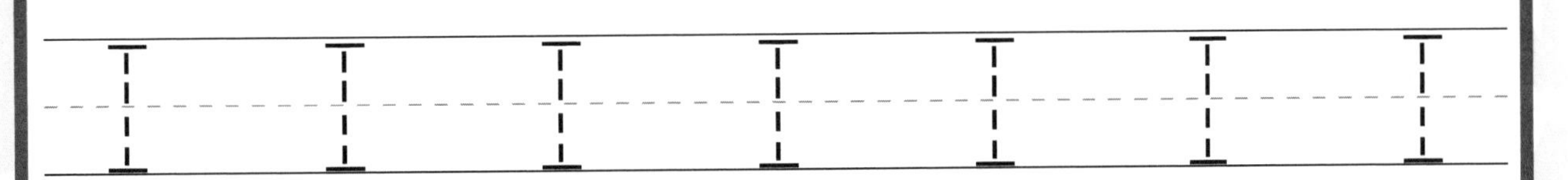

Activity Time

Find the word **can**. Draw a line under each one.

Find the word **I**. Circle each one.

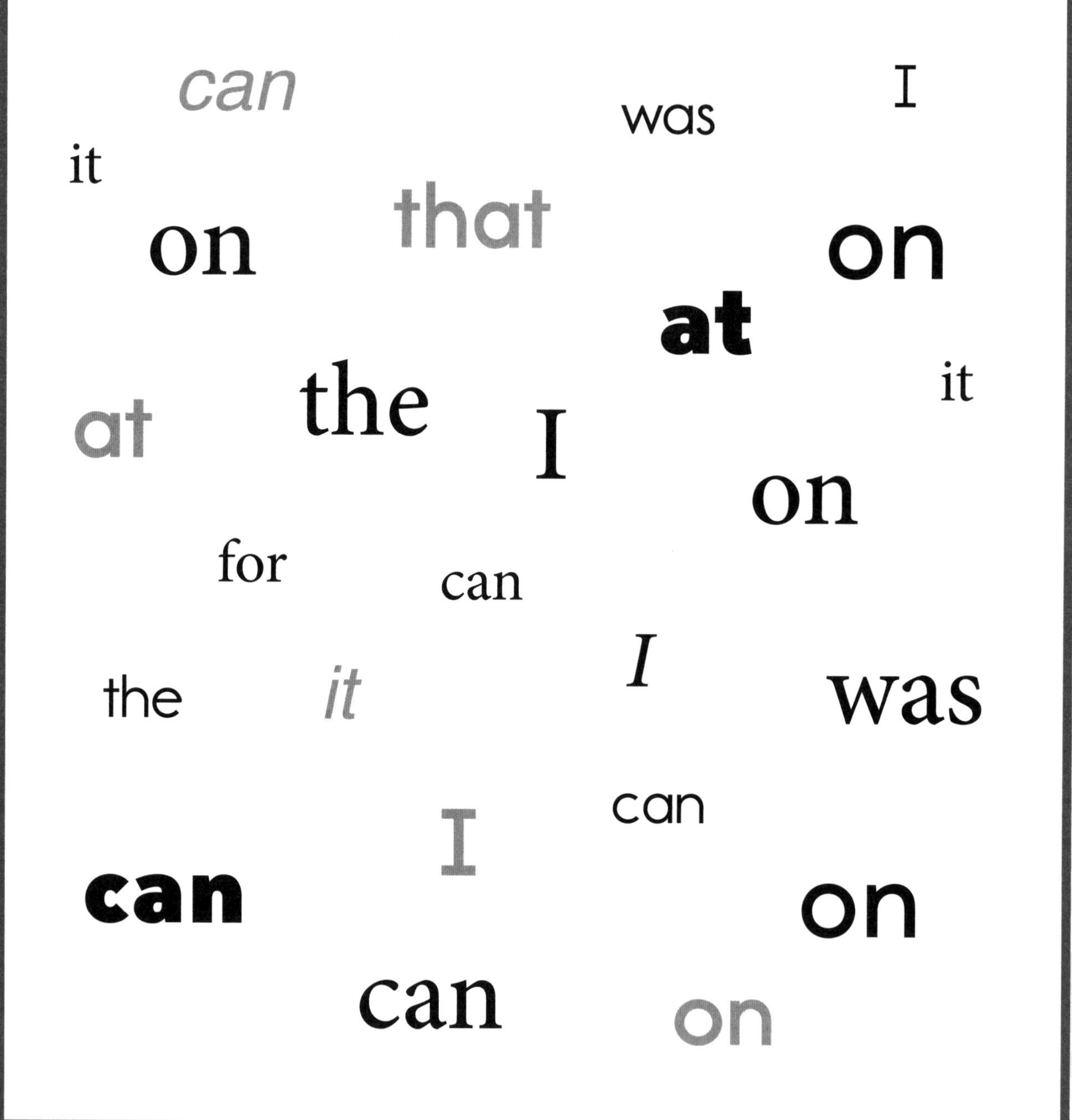

Seashells

FOCUS SIGHT WORDS:

he, she

She finds one.

He finds two.

She finds three.

He finds four.

She finds five.

They go find some more!

Activity Time

Say the word. Then, trace the word.

he he he he

he he he he

he he he he

Say the word. Then, trace the word.

she she she she

she she she she

she she she she

Activity Time

Color each circle that has the word **he** or **she**.
Then, follow the colored circles to complete the maze.

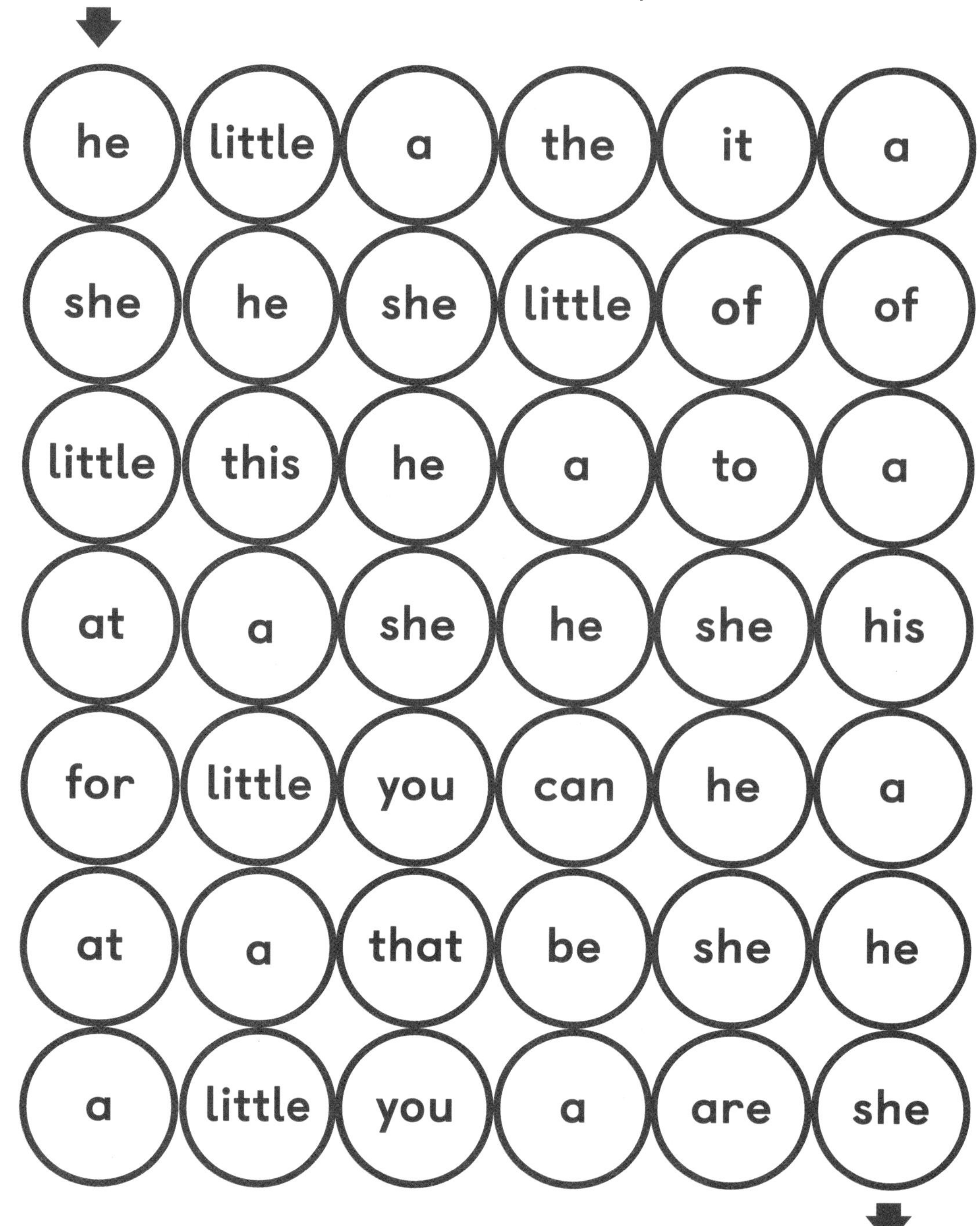

The Library

FOCUS SIGHT WORDS:

that, there

Let's go there.

There are so many.

Can I see that?

I want that one.

We go over there.

I like it there.

Activity Time

Say the word. Then, trace the word.

that that that

that that that

that that that

Say the word. Then, trace the word.

there there there

there there there

there there there

Activity Time

Color each peach that has the word **that** or **there**.

The Old House

FOCUS SIGHT WORDS:

see, will

Will you go see?

I will go see.

What will we see in there?

Look in here. See?

We will have fun.

We will come back!

Activity Time

Say the word. Then, trace the word.

Say the word. Then, trace the word.

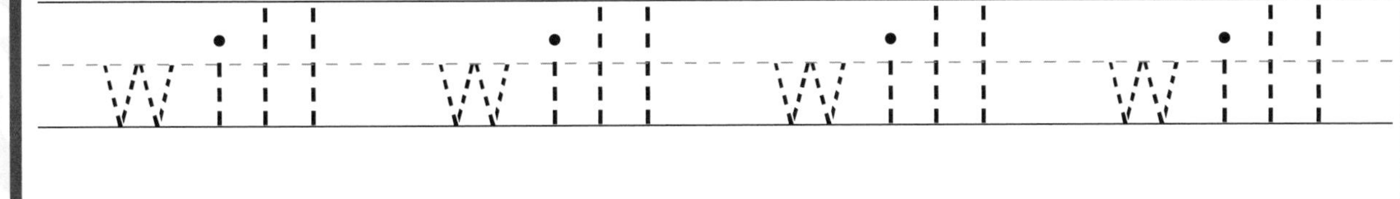

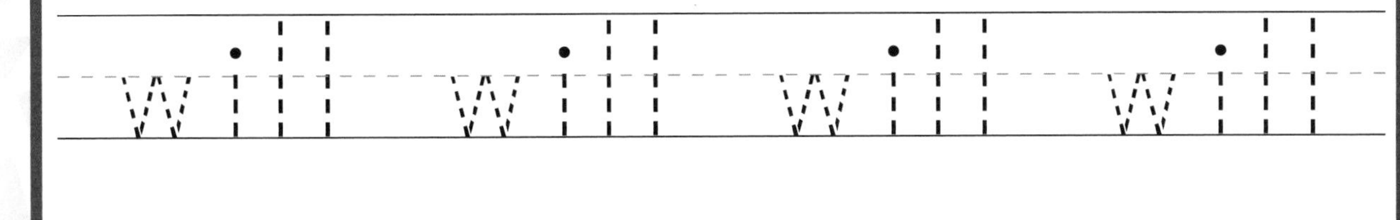

Activity Time

Find and circle the word **see** three times.
Then, do the same for the word **will**.

a w a g k a
w i l l s o
e l s e e f
t l a r e m
u h b s e e
w i l l k t

The Toy Store

FOCUS SIGHT WORDS:
this, want

What do I want?

I want this.

What do you want? This?

How about this?

I want this!

This is fun.

Activity Time

Say the word. Then, trace the word.

this this this this

this this this this

this this this this

Say the word. Then, trace the word.

want want want

want want want

want want want

Activity Time

Find the word **this**. Draw a line under each one.

Find the word **want**. Circle each one.

the want **of**

on was

the to it

this

at this

on

want **at** goes

on it

on was

this on *this* on

want was

At the Game

FOCUS SIGHT WORDS:

could, it

I could **hear** it.

I could **smell** it.

I could **taste** it.

I could **catch** it.

Could I see my team win?

Yes, I could!

Activity Time

Say the word. Then, trace the word.

could could could

could could could

could could could

Say the word. Then, trace the word.

it it it it it

it it it it it

it it it it it

Activity Time

Find and circle the word **could** three times.
Then, do the same for the word **it**.

a	b	a	g	k	c
c	o	u	l	d	o
i	p	i	y	e	u
t	d	t	r	e	l
u	c	o	u	l	d
l	k	b	i	t	t

Growing a Garden

FOCUS SIGHT WORDS:

many, time

Time to dig.

How many seeds?

Time for water.

How many days?

Time to eat!

There are many for me.

Activity Time

Say the word. Then, trace the word.

many many many

many many many

many many many

Say the word. Then, trace the word.

time time time

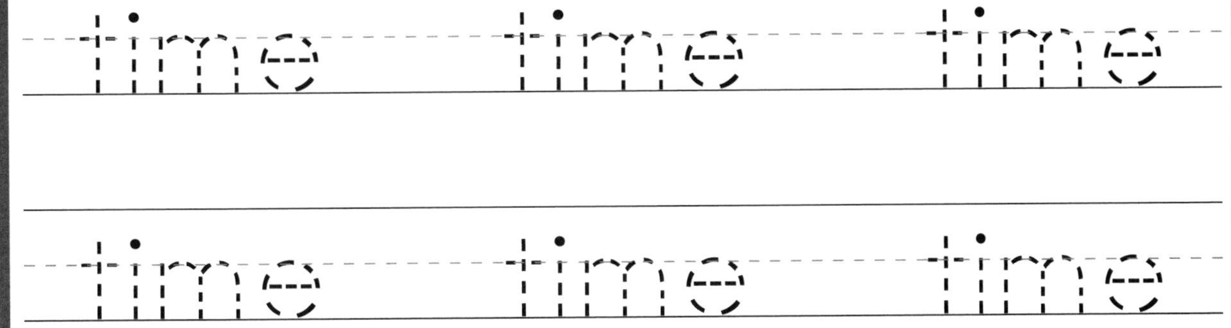

Activity Time

Color each circle that has the word **many** or **time**. Then, follow the colored circles to complete the maze.

The Lemonade Stand

FOCUS SIGHT WORDS:

we, need

We need our cart.

We need our table.

What else do we need?

Do you need this?

We need to be ready!

We need to make more!

Activity Time

Say the word. Then, trace the word.

we we we we

we we we we

we we we we

Say the word. Then, trace the word.

need need need

need need need

need need need

Activity Time

Color each space that has the word **we** or **need**.

Rainy Day Fun

FOCUS SIGHT WORDS:

go, out

Can I go out?

Yes, I can go out!

I can jump, jump, jump. It is fun.

Can I go down?

Yes, I can go down!

Now, we can go up, up, up again!

Activity Time

Say the word. Then, trace the word.

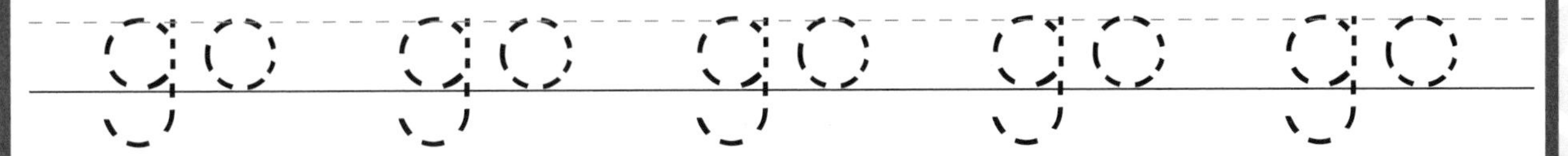

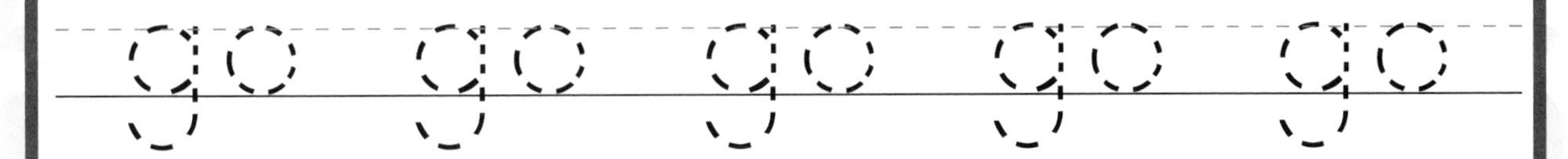

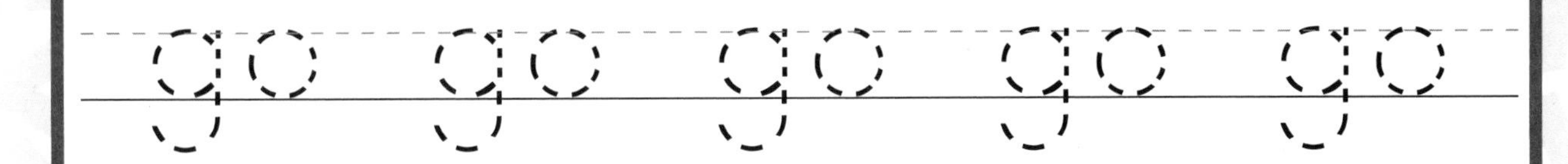

Say the word. Then, trace the word.

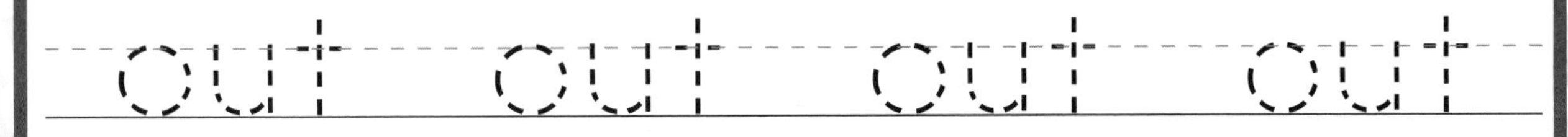

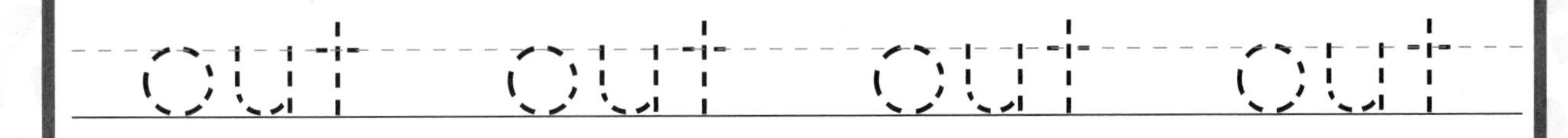

Activity Time

Color each apple that has the word **go** or **out**.

Camping

FOCUS SIGHT WORDS:

do, know

Do you know what to do?

I know how to do this.

Do you know what to do?

I know how to do this.

Do you know what to do?

I know what we can do!

Activity Time

Say the word. Then, trace the word.

do do do do do

do do do do do

do do do do do

Say the word. Then, trace the word.

know know know

know know know

know know know

Activity Time

Draw lines to connect the letters to form the word **do**.

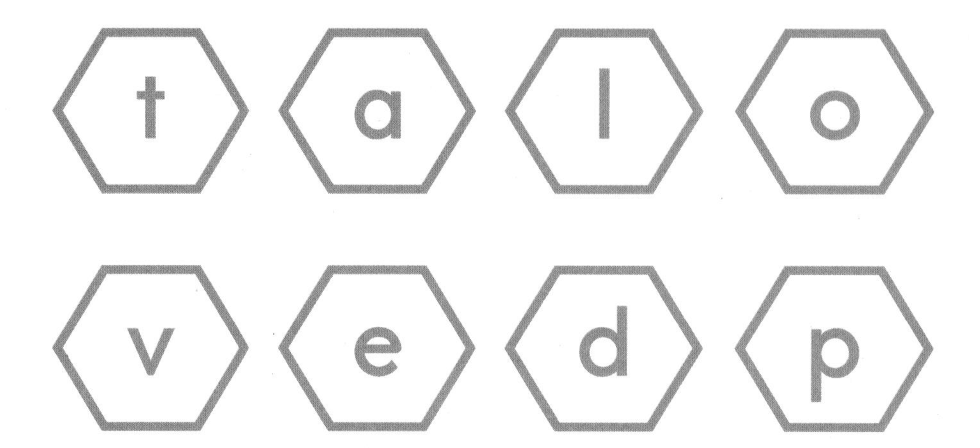

Draw lines to connect the letters to form the word **know**.

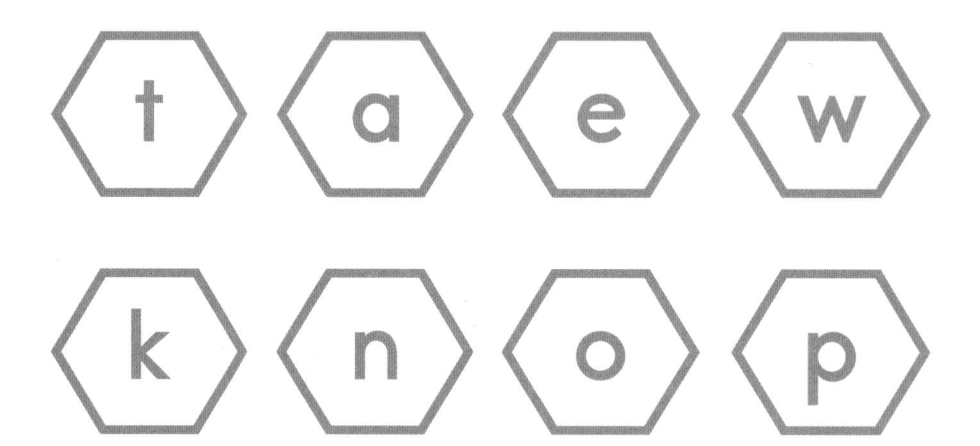

School Day

FOCUS SIGHT WORDS:

day, get

This is how our day begins.

Now, we get to work.

It is pizza day!

We get to play, too.

Now, we get ready to go home.

This is how our day ends.

Activity Time

Say the word. Then, trace the word.

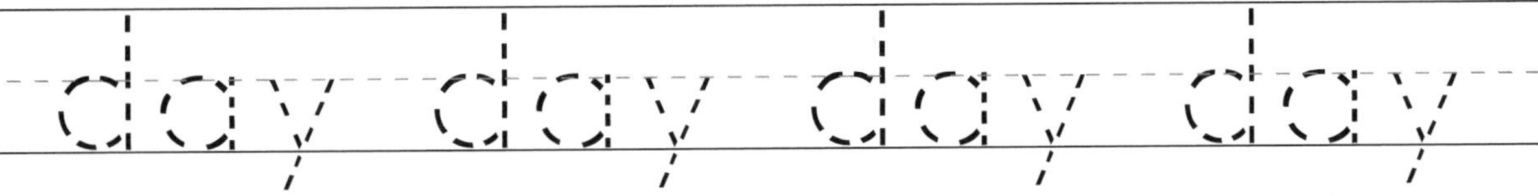

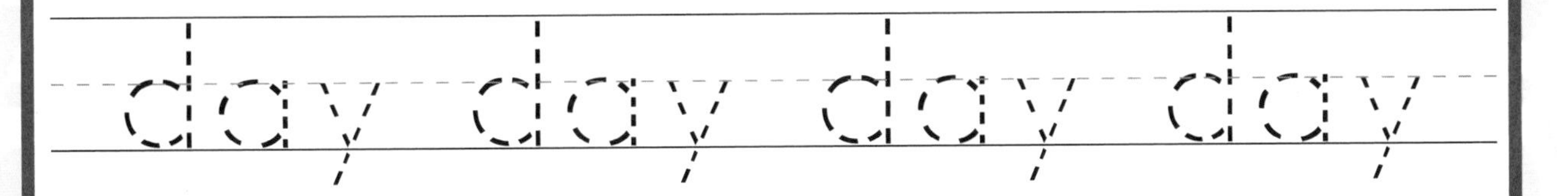

Say the word. Then, trace the word.

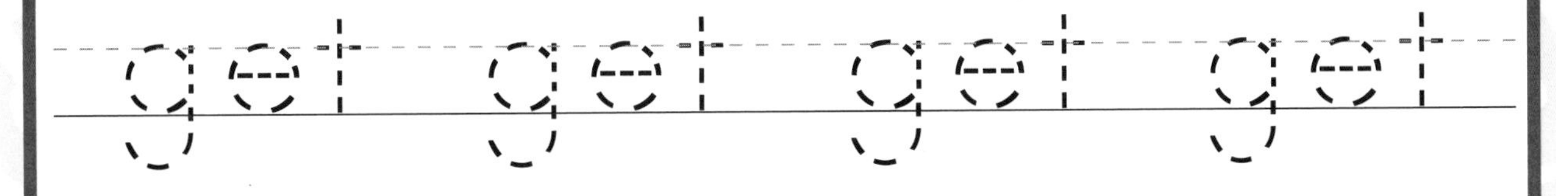

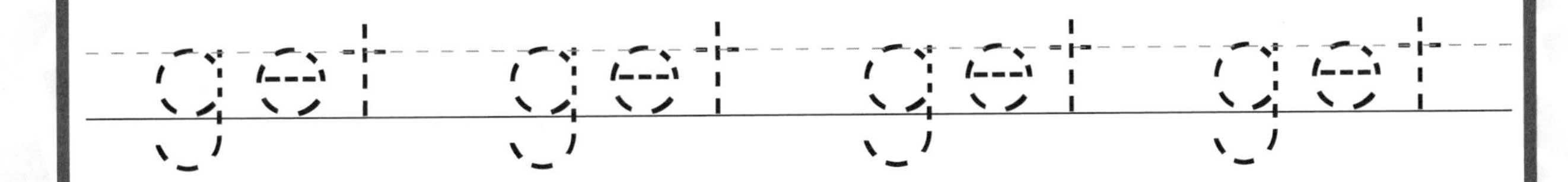

Activity Time

Find and circle the word **day** three times.
Then, do the same for the word **get**.

a	b	a	g	k	g
g	d	a	y	m	e
e	a	o	y	e	t
t	y	a	g	e	t
u	h	b	s	z	a
e	t	d	a	y	t

We Can Make It

FOCUS SIGHT WORDS:
make, they

They **want to** make **something.**

They **can** make **a boat.**

They can make a car.

What else can they do?

They can help.

Look what they can make!

Activity Time

Say the word. Then, trace the word.

make make make

make make make

make make make

Say the word. Then, trace the word.

they they they

they they they

they they they

Activity Time

Color each space that has the word **make** or **they**.

Bike Ride

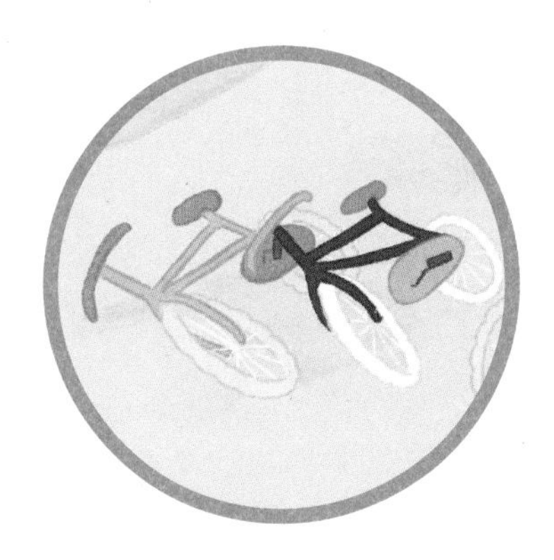

FOCUS SIGHT WORDS:

ride, should

Where should we ride?

We should ride there.

Now, where should we ride?

We should ride here.

Where should we ride next?

We should stay here!

Activity Time

Say the word. Then, trace the word.

ride ride ride

ride ride ride

ride ride ride

Say the word. Then, trace the word.

should should

should should

should should

Activity Time

Find the word **ride**. Draw a line under each.

Find the word **should**. Circle each one.

should was of

on the on

at for that

should

it

should

ride was

on

ride on goes

a of on

ride

Ocean Surprise

SIGHT WORDS:

said, away

The shark said, "Hi!"
The fish said, "Bye."
It swam away.

The shark said, "Hello!"
The whale said, "Uh-oh!"
It swam away.

The shark said, "Want to play?"
The seahorse said, "Not today."
It swam away.

The shark said, "Hey, wait!"
The octopus said, "Got to skate."
It swam away.

**“Want to go to the bay?”
asked the stingray.**

They all said, “Happy Birthday!”

Activity Time

Say the word. Then, trace the word.

said said said

said said said

said said said

Say the word. Then, trace the word.

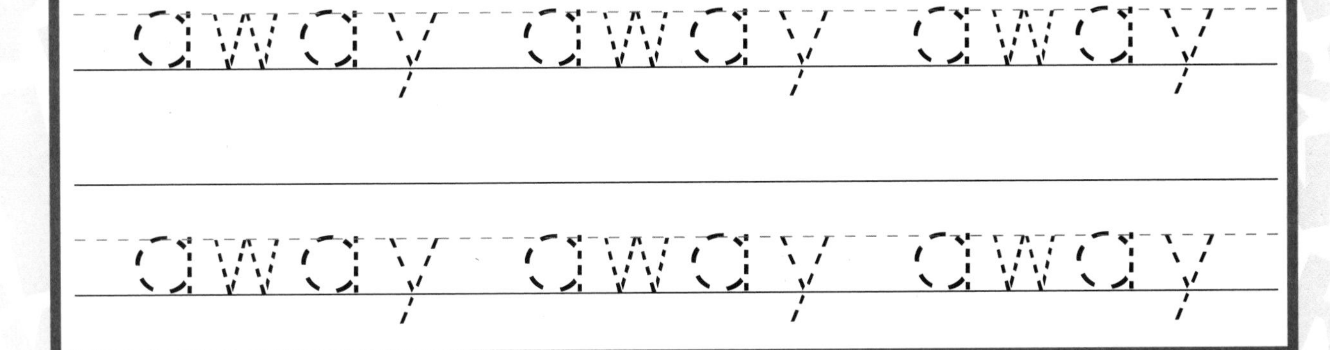

Activity Time

Draw lines to connect the letters to form the word **said**.

Draw lines to connect the letters to form the word **away**.

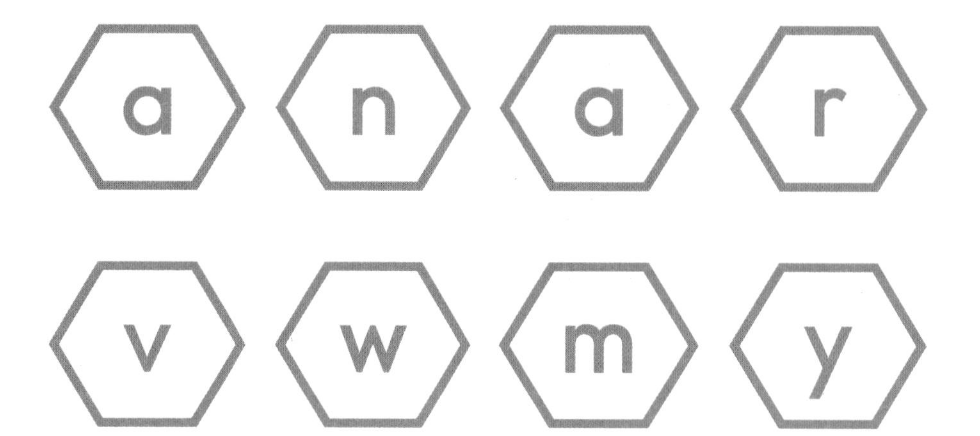

Sight Words Index

About the Author

Kimberly Ann Kiedrowski is a former kindergarten teacher of almost 10 years. She currently stays home with her son and twin daughters. She loves to share her teaching ideas on her blog. Along with blogging, she creates resources for teachers to use in their classrooms. She holds a bachelor of science degree in early childhood education from the University of Wisconsin–Green Bay.

About the Illustrator

Claire Keay lives in an old market town in the south of England with her two sons and two cats. Formerly a children's nursery nurse for many years, she moved to become an illustrator about 8 years ago—and loves her job! When not drawing you can find her singing in her local community choir or going on long countryside rambles with friends.